COLOUR
by
DESIGN

Creating Style with Paint

CREATIVE
PUBLISHING
international

MINNETONKA, MINNESOTA

Colour by Design
Created by: The Editors of Creative Publishing international, Inc.,
in cooperation with Premier Paints of Canada.

5900 Green Oak Drive
Minnetonka, MN 55343
1-800-328-3895

President: Iain Macfarlane
Vice President, Custom Services: Sue Riley
Group Director, Book Development: Zoe Graul
Director, Creative Development: Lisa Rosenthal
Executive Managing Editor: Elaine Perry
Director, Custom Marketing and Publishing:
Hugh Kennedy

Project Manager: Amy Friebe
Senior Art Director: Stephanie Michaud
Senior Editor: Linda Neubauer
Writer: Barbara Knox
Copy Editor: Janice Cauley
Prop Stylist: Coralie Sathre
Sample Production Manager:
Elizabeth Reichow
Artisans: Sharon Ecklund,
Phyllis Galbraith
Technical Photo Stylist: Bridget Haugh
Studio Services Manager:
Marcia Chambers
Photo Services Coordinator:
Carol Osterhus
Photographer: Chuck Nields
Photography Assistants: Andrea Rugg, Greg Wallace
Set Builder: Dan Widerski
Photo Researcher: Angie Spann
Mac Designer: Laurie Kristensen
Production Manager: Patt Sizer
Account Manager: John Fletcher

Photography Credits: ©Balthazar Korab, Ltd. (pp. 7, 14-15, 46-47); ©Jeff Krueger (p. 69); ©Karen Melvin/Alison Drake
Interior Design/Randall Kipp, Architect (cover, pp. 44-45); ©Karen Melvin/Anderson Master Builders (pp. 30-31);
©Karen Melvin/Ken Fearing Interior Finishes (p. 35); ©Karen Melvin/Pam Powell, St. Paul, MN (pp. 36-37); ©Karen
Melvin/Alison Drake Interior Design (p. 49); ©Karen Melvin/Landform (p. 70); ©Robert Perron/Judith Griffin Interiors
(p. 5); ©Robert Perron/Peix & Partners (p. 15).

Printed by R. R. Donnelley & Sons Co., USA.
 03 02 01 00 99 / 5 4 3 2 1

CONTENTS
table of

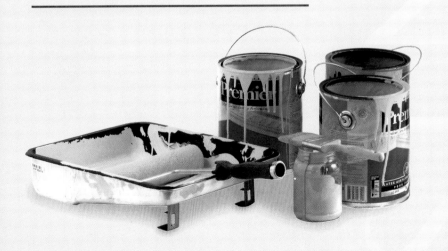

A World of Colour

Colour is the visual spice of life: it excites, soothes, entertains, and heals. You enjoy and employ the effects of colour in the clothes you wear, in the furnishings you buy, and in the flower gardens you tend. So why limit your colour selection to white or beige when it comes to painting your home?

Today, with a rainbow of paint colours available and clever decorating tools like the Premier Collection colour system to help guide your choices, colour is one of the most inexpensive luxuries your money can buy. Review some colour basics to boost your courage, then start transforming your boring rooms into showplaces that feature your favourite hues.

Contrasting sunny yellow with muted green creates a room full of drama and sophistication.

 Herbs

 Duckling

 Limelight

how colour works

CHAPTER 1

Understanding colour starts with understanding your own colour preferences. Check your closet. Often your favourite colours for clothes are the ones that make your skin, hair, and eyes most attractive. Think of your favourite paintings. Perhaps they attract you because their colour combinations lift your spirits or simply fascinate you.

Many colour experts believe that painting your home with your favourite colours can be therapeutic, just as it may be uncomfortable or difficult to live with someone else's colour choices. An understanding of how colours work and the powerful effects they have will help you develop successful colour schemes for your home.

Chantilly

Poppy

A simple two-tone monochromatic palette with a high degree of value contrast emphasizes the stylized architecture of this room.

Hundreds of years ago, Sir Isaac Newton arranged the colours, or hues, of the spectrum in a circular pattern called the colour wheel. This simple tool illustrates clearly how colours relate to one another. These basic colour terms explain what the eye sees when looking at the colour wheel:

the colour wheel

primary colours

These three hues—red, yellow, and blue— are the foundation of the world of colour. Used in their pure form, with no white or black added, these colours pack a powerful visual message.

secondary colours

Mixing equal amounts of two primary colours results in a secondary colour. Combine blue and yellow to get green; combine red and yellow to get orange; combine blue and red to get purple.

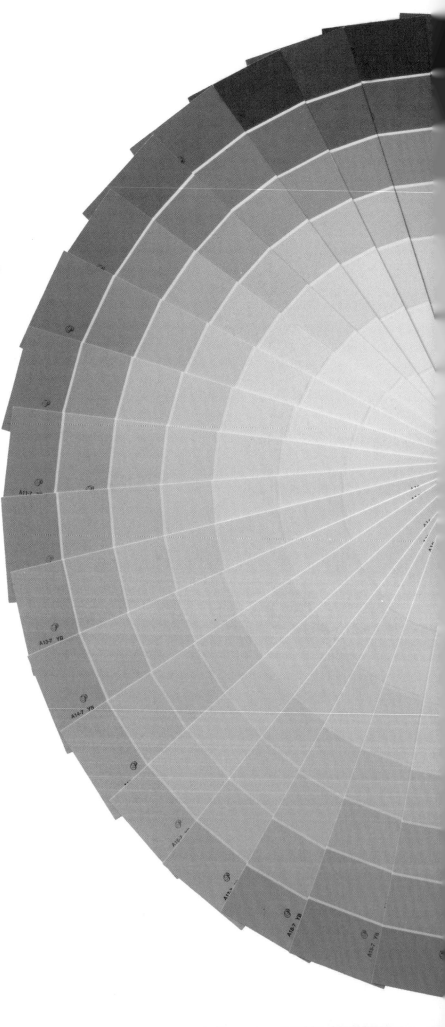

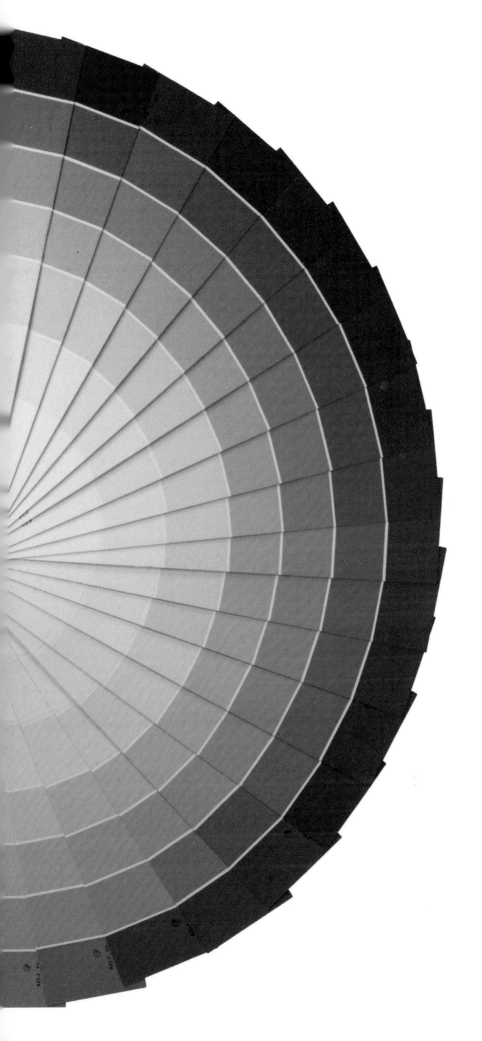

tertiary colours

Blending primary colours with secondary colours creates tertiary colours. These hues, which are less visually demanding, form the basis of many decorating palettes.

complementary colours

Colours that fall opposite one another on the colour wheel are called complementary colours. Complementary hues contrast each other visually and work naturally as great colour companions.

adjacent or analogous colours

Colours that appear next to each other on the colour wheel tend to harmonize nicely. As a general rule, an effective adjacent colour scheme is drawn from a section of the wheel that includes several tertiary hues, but no more than one primary and one secondary hue.

It's So Easy

The Premier Collection colour system has expanded the colour wheel to 1330 colours and arranged them in 38 rows and 5 columns, with the Slide Guide™ along one side. To create successful colour schemes, simply start by choosing one favourite colour!

Choosing a Monochromatic Palette. Each row shows you 35 different values and degrees of muting for a single hue. Let's say you want to develop a blue colour scheme. Simply select your favourite blue hue from the first column. In the Premier Collection, you can instantly see 35 different variations of that blue across the row, ranging from light to dark, pure to muted. To create a striking monochromatic scheme for your room, select two, three, even four choices from that same row, and the colours are guaranteed to work together.

Choosing a Complementary Palette. The 38 rows divide naturally into warm colours and cool colours between rows 19 and 20. Each row in the top half has a complementary row in the bottom half. You can quickly create a complementary scheme using the Slide Guide™. Simply align one arrow of the Slide Guide™ to a preferred colour row, perhaps a blue. The other arrow on the Slide Guide™ will automatically point to its complementary row 19 rows away, an orange row. Pick one or more of the choices from each row, and you've created a fail-safe complementary colour scheme.

It's that simple.

Once you've located the colour strips you want, take samples home and view them in their intended setting. When you've made your decisions, the store will mix them for you, following precisely measured recipes.

monochromatic

C37	B37	C25	E25	A6

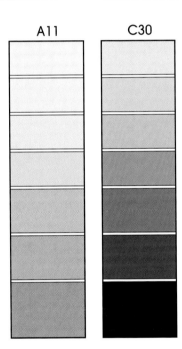

Each row in the Premier Collection holds 35 colour choices per hue. The purest colours are on strip A; the most muted on strip E, with 7 colour values from lightest to darkest on each strip. Select colours from within the same row for a monochromatic scheme. Variation in colour value and the degree of muting creates interest within the scheme.

complementary

Arrows on the Slide Guide™ indicate colour rows that are 19 rows apart; complementary rows. One row will always be warm colours; the other cool colours. Develop your scheme by selecting colours from both rows, with similar or different values and degrees of muting. Complementary colours used side by side naturally enhance each other.

A11	C30	B3	D22

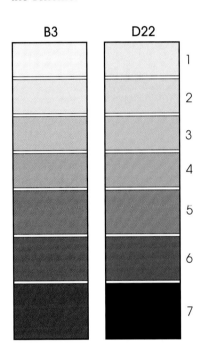

triadic (left)

Triadic schemes include colours from three families located equal distances (12 to 13 rows) apart.

adjacent (right)

Neighbouring rows within a 10- to 12-row span are used together harmoniously. The Premier Collection palette, like the colour wheel, is continuous; row 38 and row 1 are neighbours.

C38	D25	B12

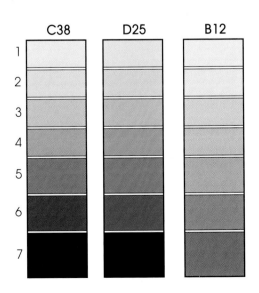

A26	B23	B14

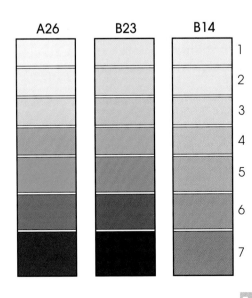

defining colours

While the colour world organizes itself neatly around the colour wheel, resulting in many helpful colour rules, there are still other factors to consider. These terms help define the subtleties of hue, and often appear in colour descriptions.

• Purity. Very pure, or saturated, colours appear clear and bright, and tend to energize interior spaces. Less saturated colours, or muted colours, are often called neutrals—greys, beiges and browns—which infuse a space with a greater sense of calm and sophistication.

• Value. Colour can change drastically based on its "lightness" or "darkness." Light colours, generally called pastels, are soothing and gentle, like the soft pink of old-fashioned roses. These soft shades are invaluable decorating tools, used to open up tiny or dark spaces, and to create soothing, welcoming rooms.

 Gallery

 Edmonston

 Underbrush

Colour values are most apparent when you are judging shades of the same hue. The lightness or darkness of these pillows, for instance, is quite obvious. The variety of colour values is what gives this grouping interest and allows you to focus on each pillow individually.

You can almost feel the energy from these bright colours. Viewed against white, they seem to bounce right off the page!

basic colour rules

WARM ROOM

Colour has a powerful impact on our lives. It can affect our emotions and energy levels, influence our perceptions of temperature and space, and even create a sense of order or chaos. Reds and oranges, for instance, actually stimulate appetite and conversation. Colour can make a room feel formal or informal, masculine or feminine, sophisticated or playful.

Using these basic rules as a guide, you can find ways to make colour work its magic in your home.

• Warm colours (reds, yellows, and oranges) appear cheerful and uplifting, while cool hues (blues, greens, and violets) are calming. Choosing the right warm or cool colours can bring a sense of well-being and harmony into your home.

• Any colour appears more intense when seen next to white. This allows you to pump up the effect of even the softest colour shades. If you favour pastels, simply paint your trim a clean white, and even the palest pink holds its own.

• Complementary colours (colours that appear opposite one another on the colour wheel) appear more intense when used side by side. For optimum results, use more of one complementary colour than the other, allowing one to dominate and the other to play a supporting role.

COOL ROOM

• Light/dark colour combinations intensify the effect of both. Because light colours advance and dark colours recede, pairing light with dark in the same room creates dramatic spaces that are visually stimulating. This effect can also work to manipulate space. For instance, an uncomfortably high ceiling can be visually lowered by painting it darker than the walls in the room.

• Always view colour samples in their intended setting, in both natural and artificial light. Northern exposures, which receive only indirect light, can benefit from bolder, brighter colours. Direct sunlight entering a room from the south tends to intensify colours and adds a subtle wash of yellow. Incandescent light emphasizes the warm colours in a room; fluorescent lighting tends to bring out the cool colours.

classic colour schemes

Designers develop rich, dramatic colour palettes based on their clients' preferences, personalities, and favourite artwork or furnishings.

NATURAL

Everglade

Muted green walls provide a gentle background for viewing some of nature's more vibrant colours.

Blonde Wood

Brittle

Fresh Drop

A monochromatic scheme was developed with varying degrees of darkness and intensity of the same hue. A pale wash of the colour on the wall unites the other elements.

natural colours

Natural colour palettes allow you to enjoy nature's glorious colours inside your home. Select your favourite season or scenic view, perhaps, and gather samples of colour from it to develop your indoor palette. For example, the warm yellows, golds, and brick reds of autumn leaves are emphasized by a brilliant blue sky. You have the basis for a natural warm colour scheme with a cool accent. The freshness of forest greenery might be the basis for a crisp monochromatic scheme.

monochromatic colours

Start with your favourite colour, and build your colour scheme with various tones and values of that hue on walls, trim, furnishings, and window treatments. Add drama by sponging or spattering a darker value of your colour on top of a lighter value, or use the various shades together in a stencil pattern. The overall effect, which can range from subdued to lively, depending on your colour choice, will be cohesive and appealing.

whites

An interior design colour classic akin to no other, white has anchored more successful rooms—indeed, whole houses—than any other single hue. The many shades of white work for decorating styles that range from English country to urban chic. Because whites are created in any colour of the rainbow, an all-white palette is developed following the same basic rules as one using full-bodied hues.

Dinner Mint

Directly opposite colours are used in different degrees of light and dark.

Apres Ski

Green Tea

complementary colours

Colours that appear opposite one another on the colour wheel form the basis for a successful complementary colour scheme. Easily selected from the Premier Collection colour system, opposite hues in varying values combine to create dramatic effects.

Apache

Blue Jazz

Muted colours can be used with pure colours in a complementary scheme.

COMPLEMENTARY COLOURS

COMPLEMENTARY COLOURS

white as an accent

Petawawa   Destiny

COLOUR + WHITE

The drama of deep muted green walls, above, is strengthened by accenting with grey-white mouldings. At left, a creamy white accents the dark red walls.

Sometimes simplicity is the way to go. This fail-safe approach works no matter what colour you choose to pair with white. Use a rich warm colour accented with white to energize a living room, a sophisticated muted green with white for the family room, or a cheerful yellow with white for the dining room. The end results are always crisp and fresh-looking.

Tandoori   Falafel

contrasting colours

Pairing light and dark colours in a decorating scheme is an approach that creates instant drama and energy. Black with white is a classic combination. Navy blue with cream, deep terracotta with pale tan, and dark grey with pale pewter are other typical examples. The hues in the scheme may be monochromatic or complementary; it is the difference in their values that creates the excitement. Dramatic contrasting schemes can revitalize the social areas of your home, the rooms where your family and friends get together.

White walls provide a perfect backdrop for bold accent colours used in furnishings and artwork.

Garbanzo Bean

decorating
with colour

CHAPTER 2

Colour helps you add your personal
touch and express your decorating
style. You may opt for a natural
scheme, bringing the colours of the
great outdoors into your home. Or,
you and your home may be well-
suited for the time-tested, traditional
approach of classic colours. Soft,
understated colour schemes can
instill quiet and calm. On the other
hand, if you want to fill your rooms
with energy, try bold, bright colours.

SOFT

NATURAL

BOLD

CLASSIC

naturals

Colours found in nature are brought inside to add depth and beauty to every room. Some natural colours, found in wood, stone, or seashells, for instance, are soft and muted, instilling quiet sophistication into the room. Others may be more lively, like a blue autumn sky, lush leaf green, or deep berry red.

The natural colour scheme in this room may have begun with the marble around the fireplace. Light, dark, and medium values, from the metals, woods, and leather, create interest and depth.

Mashed Potatoes

Frites

decorative effects

A natural colour palette may include special-effects techniques that transform a room from plain and simple to truly spectacular. Faux finishes that imitate natural surfaces – stones, woodgrains, antiqued metals – are easy to achieve with paints.

Chick Pea   Cool Mint

Closely related hues in various shades are sponged on the wall in a masked-off diamond pattern. The effect is soft and dimensional.

Light Toast

Capellini

Creme Caramel

Brandy Shake

Sponging and other texturizing techniques are used to apply multiple colours in layers, imitating the natural look of marbles, granites, and semiprecious stones.

natural paint finishes

Painted finishes mix fantasy and reality to produce dramatic results. You can paint realistic-looking aged finishes, or simply create visual texture and depth with techniques like sponging or rag rolling. Warm earthy hues used in these paint finishes help develop a natural colour scheme.

Ceshire

Old Clay

Green Pepper

Shaker boxes are colourwashed in rich earthtone colours.

 Gaspé

 Muffin

Rag rolling gives a wall dramatic texture and depth.

classic
colours

Rich muted colour accents in a
predominantly white room is a
classic palette for many upscale
interiors. Classic colours also
include sophisticated neutrals, like
grey, tan, taupe, and sand, often
used for walls in rooms where the
furnishings and artwork play a
dominant role in the scheme. Other
classic schemes include deep, rich
reds, golds, and blues, so common
in traditional decorating.

The rich muted colours of metals,
used in lamps and other
accessories, reinforce the upscale
look of warm white interiors.

Deep, moody accent colours dramatize the multi-tone whites of the walls, window treatments, and furnishings.

Chick Pea

Water Chestnut

Liberia

The muted natural colours in this high-style monochromatic room range in value, keeping your eye moving from one area to the next.

31

colour
contrast

Pair a soft, light colour with an almost-black shade and watch the drama unfold. While black and white is the classic high-contrast colour scheme, similar effects can be achieved when pale tints are used with deep colours like navy blue or deep, rich brown. To create truly dramatic, eye-catching colour schemes, it is necessary to consider all the elements in a room: furnishings, art, window treatments, and accessories. By painting the walls, ceiling, and trim in a monochromatic white palette, for instance, the furnishings and accessories can supply the contrasting punch of colour.

Hint of Oatmeal   Oatmeal   Pincourt

Warm white paired with a cool dark colour heightens the contrast.

Picasso Blue

Gold

Metallic gold
accessories intensify
the impact of a dark
blue wall.

Cream of
Potato

Old Clay

Adjacent hues used
in high-contrast
values form a
satisfying mix for this
wall arrangement.

elegant classics

Timeless classics, like navy blue, forest green, burgundy, and gold are the foundation for many elegant colour schemes. The hallmark of traditional decorating style, these colours fill a room with a sense of stability, tastefulness, and old-world charm.

New Pine

Soft gold walls set a welcoming backdrop in a home with traditional styling and classic dark wood tones.

To create a sophisticated, classic colour scheme, select deep colours as a stunning backdrop for furnishings and accessories. To add more visual drama to a room, contrast the rich colour with a warm white.

Red, blue, and yellow, the primary colours, used together in deep tones are a great mix for a traditional bedroom.

Oxide

Dijon

soft colours

Gentle, soft, and breezy, pastel colours love the light and never overwhelm a room. They help lighten dark corners and add a feeling of spaciousness.

The cool serenity of a muted green coupled with warm white establishes a soft, quiet atmosphere for this children's bedroom.

Hint of Oatmeal   Dried Moss

LARKSPUR

Philodendron

Pastel green walls are accented with almost white trim in a monochromatic scheme.

Purdy Ivory   Creme Caramel

A whisper-warm undercoat, followed by a colour wash in a slightly darker shade, softens the texture of a stucco wall.

soft colour with a kick

When you create a pastel colour palette, consider adding a little punch with a medium colour. Muted pastels used for large areas, like walls and floors, gain momentum when a pure accent colour is added to the mix.

Cool, pale, muted green floor and walls are accented with a pillow in an adjacent pure hue that has a darker value.

Green Grocer   Tarragon

A pure accent colour used in the chair cushion adds a little pizzazz to an understated complementary scheme.

Yellow Brick   Cool Blue   Hazy Blue

many faces of white

Dockside

Oatmeal

An assortment of warm whites creates an inviting atmosphere for a breakfast nook.

Sunshine magnifies the warm tones of a white room, below.

Liberia

Crepe

Pistachio Cream

Silver Bird

Cool whites work well in the bathroom, left. Using warm whites for the towels tempers the coolness and enriches the palette.

Select two or three whites, using one for wall colour, a second for trim, and a third for ceilings. Kitchens and bathrooms are great candidates for white schemes. Look for moisture-resistant latex enamel paints specially formulated for kitchens and baths.

bold colours

Bold, vibrant colours enliven a room with excitement and energy. These pure hues brighten and refresh an area, drawing all eyes in their direction. Complementary bold colours used together add startling drama, while various colour values and subtle background colours add to the success of the scheme.

Walls are painted a warm shade of Butterscotch, the perfect complement to showcase this stunning violet settee.

Butterscotch

Alyssa and Raisin contribute to the success of this bold adjacent scheme.

 Alyssa

 Raisin

adjacent & triadic bolds

Colour schemes that include several neighbouring hues are called adjacent, or analogous. They may include several tertiary colours, one primary, and one secondary colour.

Another successful colour scheme uses *triads,* three colours that are spaced equal distances apart on the colour wheel. For instance, the three primary colours, red, blue, and yellow, form a bold and playful triadic scheme. For more sophistication, use secondary or tertiary colours in muted tones for triadic schemes.

This triadic scheme uses three colours with varying degrees of purity to give the arrangement a rich, upscale appearance.

Clay Pot

Life Green

Pansy

An adjacent scheme, built around various shades of yellow and green, is accented with other bold colours for an eclectic look.

Juniper   Sunburst

bold colour

Try something exciting and bold with bright, saturated colours that look new and uninhibited. The vibrancy of saturated colours like blue or yellow can wake up tired rooms instantly.

St. Andrews

Bold blue walls can't help but energize your morning. Echoing the ocean blue view, the look is crisp and inviting. The scheme continues into the master bathroom with a boldly striped floor.

Claret

Eucalyptus

Summer Gold

With a slightly muted green backdrop, these rich jewel tones mixed with metallic gold brighten a small bathroom.

understanding paint

CHAPTER 3

There's more to know about paint
than simply what colour to buy. In
fact, you'll find all kinds of paint
formulas, each specially designed
for particular surfaces or to achieve
particular effects. Ease of application
and clean-up are things to consider,
also. What type of paint do you want
for your project? What kind of finish
will give you optimum results for the
surfaces you want to paint? How
much paint do you need? There are
some helpful guidelines on the
following pages.

Radicchio

Powder Puff

Drama and intensity
is achieved with a
monochromatic
colour scheme using
two very different
colour values.

buying paint

If you are uncertain about your colour choices, it is wise to purchase a small can of each colour first, take them home, and test them. Paint out the colours on a large sheet of poster board, and tape it to the wall. View the sample in both daylight and artificial light; consider how the colours interact with your furnishings and each other.

coverage

How much paint do you need? The paint can label gives you an estimate of the amount of wall space the paint in that can will cover. As a rough estimate, most interior paints should cover about 400 square feet per gallon (36 square metres per 3.56 litres). This estimate is fairly accurate, assuming you have prepared and primed the surfaces properly and are intending to paint only one coat. Drastic colour changes or very porous surfaces may require two coats, doubling your needs. Measure the areas (height × width = area) you intend to paint, and buy enough paint to complete the job.

timing

Allow yourself plenty of time to complete the project, and don't rush second coats. As a general rule, latex paints take 1 to 4 hours to dry to the touch and are ready for second coats after 6 hours. Alkyd paints are dry to the touch in 8 hours; second coats should be delayed for 24 hours. Expect the preparation time to take as long or longer than the actual painting.

low-lustre   semi-gloss   gloss

Alyssa

SHEEN	FLAT	LOW-LUSTRE	SEMI-GLOSS	GLOSS
appearance	soft, gentle	subtle, low glare	medium gloss	high gloss
washability	good	excellent	excellent	excellent
scrubbability	poor	good	excellent	excellent
hiding	excellent	very good	good	good
stain resistance	poor	good	very good	excellent
masks wall defects	excellent	very good	good	poor

Reflective sheens (semi-gloss and gloss) may appear slightly lighter in value than those that absorb light (low-lustre and flat). When selecting flat paint, you may wish to go a tint lighter.

surface preparation

Though you may be anxious to get to the fun part, spend the time and effort first to take care of any surface defects or problem areas. Careful preparation of the surfaces before painting results in smoother coverage and a lasting finish.

cleaning

To begin with, give the walls a thorough cleaning, using a TSP (trisodium phosphate) solution. TSP is a concentrated, water-soluble cleanser, formulated to remove grease and dirt, and it rinses without leaving a residue that could interfere with your paint finish. While you are washing, take note of any nail holes, cracks, stains, or other problems that need to be fixed before you paint. Rinse the walls thoroughly with clear water, and allow them to dry.

Painting over wallpaper is not recommended. If possible, remove it with a steamer. Thoroughly clean the walls to remove the sizing and adhesive underneath, as this will interfere with paint adhesion. Sometimes wallpaper simply cannot be removed without damaging the walls. In this case, prime the walls with an alkyd primer before painting.

Severe staining caused by water damage, mould or mildew, crayons or permanent markers requires special attention. You won't be able to simply paint over them; they'll be back to haunt you and ruin your new finish.

FOR THIS STAIN	DO THIS
water or rust stains	Find and repair the cause; repair any damaged wall surface (page 54). Seal and cover with stain barrier primer (page 56) before painting.
mildew or mould	Wash with a solution of 1 part chlorine bleach to 4 parts water; scrub with soft brush. Then wash with TSP and rinse with clear water. Allow to dry thoroughly before painting.
ink, crayon, marker, etc.	Seal and cover with stain barrier primer before painting.

minor repairs

Now is your chance to patch any little nail holes, popped drywall nails, dents, gouges, or worse. Arm yourself with spackle, putty knife, and sandpaper for most repairs. Repair larger holes with patching kits.

techniques

small holes, dents & gouges

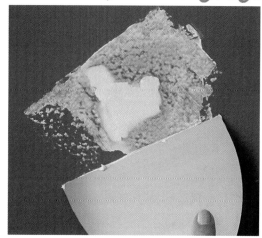

1. Sand the area free of loose paint or drywall material. Force spackle into the hole or depression with a finger or putty knife, filling it completely. Scrape the surface smooth, using the knife,

and allow it to dry.

2. Sand the area smooth with 150-grit sandpaper. Wipe it clean with a damp cloth; allow to dry, and apply primer (page 56).

techniques

popped drywall nails

1. Drive in a wallboard screw about 2" (5 cm) directly below the popped nail, countersinking the head. The screw should hit a stud and pull the drywall tight against it.

2. Scrape away any chipped paint or drywall from around the popped nail. Pound the nail back into the stud,

countersinking the head.

3. Cover the screw and nail heads with spackle. Scrape the surface smooth with a putty knife, and allow it to dry.

4. Sand the area smooth with 150-grit sandpaper. Wipe it clean with a damp cloth; allow to dry, and apply primer (page 56).

blemishes in painted wood

techniques

1. Scrape away chipped paint. Sand the area with 180-grit sandpaper until it feels smooth to the touch.

2. Fill small holes or cracks with wood

putty; allow to dry. Sand smooth.

3. Wipe wood clean with a tack cloth. Apply primer (page 56).

cracked plaster

techniques

1. Scrape away loose paint and plaster along the length of the crack. Apply self-adhesive fiberglass drywall tape over the crack to reinforce it.

2. Apply thin layers of joint compound over the taped area, hiding the tape and blending the repair

into the surrounding surface. Allow each layer to dry completely before adding the next.

3. Sand the area smooth with 150-grit sandpaper. Wipe it clean with a damp cloth; allow to dry, and apply primer (page 56).

protect the surroundings

Take care to protect any surfaces that are not to be painted, such as stained and varnished wood trim, furnishings, and light fixtures. A little effort in advance will save you a lot of trouble later and give you a more professional-looking paint job.

TIPS

• Remove all window treatments and hardware. This might be a good time to send them out to be dry-cleaned.

• Remove items like metal hardware from doors and windows, switch and outlet plates, and duct covers. Place them in plastic bags together with their screws, and label where they came from, if necessary.

• Remove the bases and shades from ceiling or wall light fixtures. Wrap fixed parts in plastic, only if you do not intend to use the light while painting.

• Move heavy furniture to the centre of the room, and cover it completely with plastic or canvas drop cloths. Don't use old sheets, as paint will soak through them.

• Cover floors with canvas drop cloths, rather than slippery plastic. Aside from the safety issue, spilled paint dries faster on canvas.

Primers, available in both latex and alkyd forms, are specialized undercoat paints. Though they may look like plain old white paint to you, primers are formulated to adhere to and seal specific surfaces, dry quickly, and provide an optimum bond between the new paint and the surface. For drastic colour changes, use a tinted primer to make the transition easier.

Because primers are not designed for durability or weather resistance, apply them just before you intend to paint. Apply the primer, using rollers, brushes, or pads, following the same tips and techniques used for painting (pages 62 to 67).

primers

When should you prime?

- When the surface has never been painted before (wood, drywall, plaster, or metal).

- Whenever you have sanded or patched the surface.

- Before applying low-lustre, semi-gloss, or gloss paint.

- When making drastic colour changes.

ON THIS SURFACE	USE THIS PRIMER
unfinished wood	alkyd primer
painted wood	latex or alkyd primer (necessary only on bare areas)
new drywall	latex primer
painted drywall	latex primer
new plaster	latex primer
painted plaster	latex primer
chalky surface or very old paint	super adherent acrylic primer
wallpaper	alkyd primer
metal	metal primer or alkyd primer
stains, water marks, knotholes	stain barrier primer

The right primer can ensure one-coat coverage, saving you money on your decorator paint. Primers also seal porous areas, like dried spackle, and provide a uniform surface to paint over. Though alkyd primer is recommended for wood, you can paint over it with latex paint.

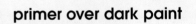

primer over dark paint

primer over drywall

The right tools, proper preparation, and quality paints are the key to successful

tools

paint projects. Invest in high-quality tools the first time. They not only produce the best finish, they are also easiest to work with and, with proper care, will last through one paint project after another.

rollers

Premium-quality paint rollers are your best friends when it comes to painting walls, ceilings, and floors. They help you cover large areas quickly and smoothly with maximum coverage and minimum effort. For painting with rollers, you need three basic parts: the roller cage, the roller cover, and the roller tray. One of each per painter is sufficient to get a one-colour job done. However, additional roller covers are essential for multi-colour applications.

A standard roller cage has several metal support ribs designed to hold a 9" (23 cm) cover. Select one with a comfortable handle, threaded to accommodate an extension pole for painting beyond your reach. Make sure it spins freely and smoothly.

The best roller covers have dense nap on plastic cores that will not warp out of shape or disintegrate like the cheaper cardboard-core covers. The nap depth is available from 6 mm to 25 mm. In general, the shorter the nap, the smoother the paint finish. Check the chart for specifics.

USE THIS NAP DEPTH	WITH THIS PAINT	FOR THIS PURPOSE
6 mm smooth	gloss or semi-gloss	smooth, reflective finish on wood or metal
10 mm semi-smooth	flat, low-lustre, or semi-gloss	slightly pebbled finish on sand-finished plaster or drywall; hides imperfections
19 mm semi-rough	flat or ceiling paint	pebbled finish; use on textured surfaces like plaster or stucco
25 mm rough	flat or masonry paint	very rough finish; use on heavily textured surfaces

brushes & pads

Paintbrushes are useful for small areas, or for places where precision is important, such as woodwork and abutting edges of walls and ceilings. Paintbrushes also fall into two basic categories: natural bristle, for use with alkyd paints, and synthetic bristle, for use with all paints. Avoid using natural-bristle brushes with latex paint, as the bristles will expand and become damaged. Look for brushes that have strong handles with firmly attached metal ferrules. High-quality brushes have long bristles with flagged, or split, ends that come to a tapered point. These features allow you to paint with fewer brush marks and apply more paint per stroke. Spacer plugs secure the bristles firmly, keeping them in the brush and not lost in your paint job.

Paint pads in various sizes and shapes are another way to apply latex paint. Though they apply paint in a thinner coat, they are convenient when you have to paint areas where a roller would be too clumsy and a brush too tedious.

USE THIS TOOL	FOR THIS PURPOSE
3" (7.5 cm) straight-edged brush	cutting in
2" or 2½" (5 or 6.5 cm) angled brush	painting narrow mouldings and window trim
2" (5 cm) straight-edged brush	painting woodwork
large standard paint pad	applying latex paint to large flat surfaces
large heavy-duty paint pad	applying exterior latex paint to lapped siding or shakes
small paint pad	applying latex paint to narrow mouldings
4" (10 cm) foam roller	applying latex paint in hard-to-reach areas, such as metal radiators or pipes

taping

Save yourself additional cleanup time or paint touch-ups by masking off woodwork before painting the walls. For best results, use painter's tape, which is a wide strip of brown paper with adhesive along one edge. Working with short sections, smooth the adhesive onto the woodwork with your fingers or a putty knife, butting the adhesive edge against the wall. The paper extends out over the moulding, protecting it from drips and spatters.

For a clean straight line at the ceiling, mask the ceiling edge with painter's tape before painting the walls. Remove the tape before the paint is completely dry to avoid lifting the paint and distorting the straight line.

Use painter's masking tape on walls to create special effects like stripes or diamonds.

draping

If you intend to paint the ceiling only, drape your walls in plastic to protect them from paint drips and spatters. Secure plastic sheeting to the walls with a strip of painter's masking tape at the ceiling line.

painting techniques &tips

There are techniques and tips for using your painting tools that will help you finish your project in the shortest time with the best results. Because you were not born knowing how to hold a paintbrush or roll a roller, here are some quick tips to get you started on the right track.

rollers

TIPS FOR PAINTING WITH ROLLERS

• Remove lint and loose nap fibers from new roller covers, using masking tape.

• Before dipping the roller into paint for the first time, moisten it with water, if you're using latex paint, or with mineral spirits, if you're using alkyd paint.

techniques

1. Pour enough paint into the tray to fill the well, but not cover the ramp.

2. Load paint onto the roller, by dipping it into the well. Then roll it back and forth on the textured ramp, distributing the paint evenly. The roller cover should be covered with paint, but not dripping, when you take it to the wall.

3. Covering a square yard (metre) of wall space, roll

the paint onto the wall in a large M or W.

4. Roll back and forth horizontally across the large letter, to distribute the paint evenly.

5. To leave a smooth, even finish, roll from top to bottom in slightly overlapping strokes, lifting the roller, and starting at the top with each stroke.

6. Repeat steps 2 to 5 in each adjacent area, always working back into wet paint.

brushes

TIPS FOR PAINTING WITH BRUSHES

• Flex the bristles of a new brush to loosen them.

• Avoid "overdipping" your brushes. Load paint onto the bottom third of the bristles only. Gently tap the brush against the inside of the can rim to remove excess paint.

techniques

1. Apply paint to a small area with horizontal strokes in a back-and-forth motion, unloading first one side of the brush and then the other. Apply just enough pressure to bend the brush tip slightly.

2. Using long vertical strokes, smooth the paint

evenly across the wet surface. Brush lightly along the edges of the painted areas with just the tip of the brush to "feather" them.

3. Repeat steps 1 and 2 in each adjacent area, always working back into wet paint for a seamless look.

pads

TIPS FOR PAINTING WITH PADS

• Fill a pad tray or pan with paint so that the pad can be floated level on the surface.

• Load paint only onto the filaments on the pad surface; avoid getting paint on the sides or top of the pad. Draw the pad gently against the tray rim to remove excess paint.

• Always pull the pad towards you on the wall; never push it away.

techniques

1. Covering a 2' × 2' (0.63 × 0.63 m) area, apply paint onto the wall in a large X. Begin at the top, and draw downwards, always pulling the pad towards you.

2. Spread the paint evenly across the area by drawing the pad horizontally in overlapping strokes. Lift the pad at the end of each stroke, and begin again at the opposite side.

3. To leave a smooth, even finish, draw downwards in light, overlapping strokes across the wet surface.

4. Repeat steps 1 to 3 in each adjacent area, always working back into wet paint.

painting
a room

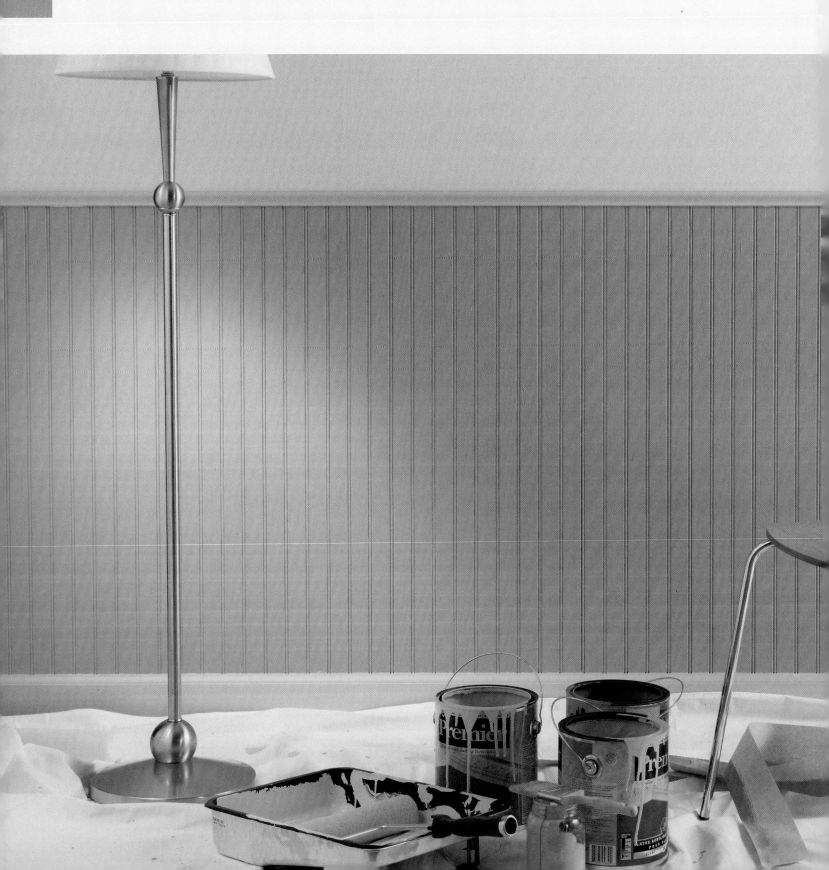

Sea Isle

Artesian

When you paint an entire room, begin with the ceiling. That way, any paint spatters that land on walls or woodwork can be cleaned up and painted over later. Paint woodwork second, and allow it to dry completely so that it can be masked off before you paint the walls.

ceilings

TIPS FOR PAINTING CEILINGS

• Start painting near a window, and work back into the room. The natural light from the window gives you a better view of your work and makes mistakes more apparent.

• Wear safety goggles to protect your eyes from paint spatters; a hat or scarf to protect your hair.

• Use on extension pole on your roller handle, so you can work from the floor, instead of climbing up and down a ladder.

1. Paint a narrow strip of paint along the outer edges of the ceiling, using a paintbrush or a paint pad 2½" to 3" (6.5 to 7.5 cm) wide. This is called "cutting in." Feather the edge towards the interior to minimize brush strokes.

2. Apply paint to the rest of the ceiling, using a roller, as in steps 1 to 6 on page 62. Begin in a corner, and work outwards into the room, one area at a time.

techniques

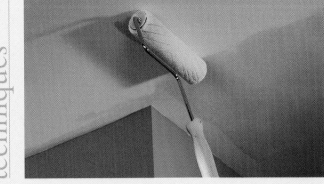

woodwork

TIPS FOR PAINTING WOODWORK

• Use a narrow sash brush, either straight or angled, for painting trim around windows and doors, baseboards, and ceiling moulding.

• Always stroke in the direction of the wood grain.

• For carved mouldings, use a stiff-bristle stencil brush. Paint in circular strokes to reach all the nooks and crannies. Then follow up with a sash brush.

• Remove windows from their frames if possible. Remove any metal hardware, rather than trying to paint around it.

• Paint windows and doors one surface at a time, in the order shown. When painting near the glass, allow a very narrow edge of paint to overlap onto the glass, forming a weather seal. Wipe excess paint from the glass, using a putty knife wrapped with a clean cloth. Or, wait until the paint dries, and remove it with a razor blade.

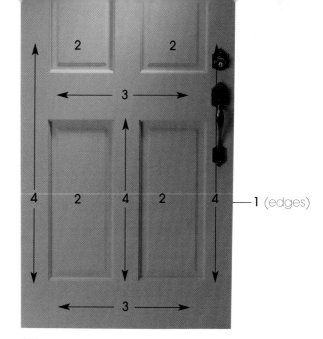

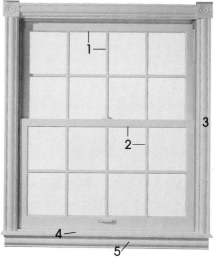

walls

TIPS FOR PAINTING WALLS

• If you are right-handed, work from right to left; if left-handed, work from left to right. This keeps your body away from the wet paint.

• Complete an entire wall before taking a break, to ensure a nice even finish.

1. Cut in carefully along the edge of the ceiling, holding the brush or pad at a slight angle. Move the brush or pad slowly along the crease to achieve a smooth, straight line. Also cut in on both sides of each corner and around all woodwork. Remember to

feather the edges of the paint line where it will be overlapped by the roller.

2. Apply paint to the rest of the wall surface, as in steps 1 to 6 on page 62. Begin in an upper corner, and work down, then across, one area at a time.

techniques

clean-up &storage

You're almost there! The painting is finished; your room looks great. The final step is clean-up. Done properly, you'll leave your tools and supplies ready for future projects or necessary touch-ups.

CLEAN-UP TIPS

• Remove masking tape before paint dries to avoid lifting paint from surface.

• Remove dried-on paint spatters from window glass, using a razor blade.

• Remove as much paint as you can from brushes and pads, simply by painting an old cardboard box. Scrape excess paint from roller covers, using a curved tool.

• Wash tools used for latex paint in soapy water; clean tools used for alkyd paints in solvent.

STORAGE TIPS

• Replace clean, dry brushes in their original cardboard wrappers or wrap in brown paper to protect the bristles. The best way to store brushes is to hang them.

• Wrap clean dry roller covers in plastic or paper; store standing on end.

• Store small amounts of leftover paints in glass jars with tight-fitting lids. Label clearly for future reference. Store larger amounts in their original containers; store tightly sealed cans upside down.

• Allow solvents used for clean-up to settle for a week. Then pour off the clear liquid into a glass jar; seal tightly, and label. Dispose of the paint residue in a manner appropriate for hazardous waste.

• There are environmentally sound ways to dispose of empty paint cans and alkyd paint residue. Check your local waste disposal program.

exterior colour strategy

CHAPTER 4

A freshly painted outer shell may be just the face-lift your home needs to make it look new again. Basic colour effects also apply to your home's exterior. For instance, light colour values and neutral tones make a house look larger; medium to dark colours shrink its perceived size. Darker trim around doors and windows can diminish the size of a house by visually dividing it into many smaller parts. You can emphasize attractive architectural features by painting them in contrasting accent colours.

Poinsetta

Radiant

Raven

Bold colours are even more striking posed against a black background. It takes a unique house with distinctive architecture to successfully carry a colour scheme like this.

• Don't use too many colours – light and dark versions of one or two colours work best.

• Use strong accent colours to enhance attractive features sparingly – the front door is usually the best feature to accentuate.

• Paint elements like downspouts, eaves, and vents the same colour as the siding or trim next to them, so they blend into the background.

• Continue your colour scheme to your attached garage, and paint the garage door the same colour as the house siding or trim.

• Choose muted colours – they look better in bright daylight and blend nicely with nature's palette.

• Consider permanent colours, such as the roof, masonry walls or fireplace chimneys, driveways, and foundation landscaping, when selecting your overall colour scheme.

• View paint samples outside in the same light your house receives and at different times during the day.

• Never paint vinyl siding darker than its original colour. The darker colour will absorb more heat, causing the siding to warp and buckle.

• Paint heavily textured stucco or wood surfaces shades lighter than you desire. Shadows produced by the texture make colours appear darker.

• Research historical colour palettes if you wish to preserve the colours of an older home.

If you're not quite sure where to start, take a drive, and look for houses similar to yours. Take note of the ones you like or strongly dislike, and analyze why.

Once you've selected colour options at the store, take the samples home and view them outdoors. Here are a few more tips to help you make your selections:

selecting colours

Sweet Butter and Parchment are actually monochromatic colours, both located in row 14. Used together, they give the house a very clean, natural look.

Sweet Butter

Parchment

Main colour: Dundas

Shutters, trim, & garage door: Landing

Front door: Velvet

Main colour: Buff

Shutters, trim, & garage door: Mocha

Front door: Whistler Sky

Main colour: Rooftile

Trim & garage door: Metropolis

Shutters: Black

Front door: Sangria

Main colour: Pizzaz

Shutters, trim, & garage door: White (ready mix)

Front door: Hunter

Main colour: Peanut Cream

Shutters, trim, & garage door: Purdy Ivory

Front door: Shutter

Main colour: Jordan

Shutters, trim, & garage door: Stratford

Front door: Wildfield

preparing the exterior

minor repairs

surface preparation

Properly preparing the exterior surfaces before you paint is the key to a successful, long-lasting exterior paint job. Unless your home is in mint condition, you can expect preparation to take longer than the actual painting. Here's a checklist of preparation tasks that may be necessary:

- Scrape away all loose, chipped, or peeling paint.

- Sand rough areas.

- Sand all weathered wood.

- Repair holes and cracks.

- Remove all old caulking; caulk all joints and cracks.

- Wash thoroughly with TSP; remove mildew with bleach, and rinse.

- Prime where necessary.

The condition of the existing paint may give you a clue about some other problems that should be dealt with before you repaint. Watch for these conditions and follow these steps to correct them.

THIS PROBLEM	IS CAUSED BY THIS CONDITION	HERE'S WHAT TO DO
alligatoring (A)	paint has dried too quickly, too many layers are built up over time, or paint was applied too thickly	Remove thick build-up with heat gun, or scrape away loose paint with wire brush or scraper; sand smooth.
peeling or chipping (B)	poor surface preparation under old paint, or degeneration of substrate (rotting wood)	Scrape away loose paint with wire brush or scraper; sand smooth. Repair damaged wood.
chalking (C)	powder film that forms on alkyd paints through prolonged exposure	Wash off with scrub brush and TSP, or power wash. Repaint.
blistering (D)	moisture is trapped under the paint	Scrape away loose paint with wire brush or scraper; sand smooth. Check for proper venting in soffits, roof.
mildew (E)	dampness; common in areas that do not receive sunlight	Wash the area with chlorine bleach solution. Check for proper venting in soffits, roof.

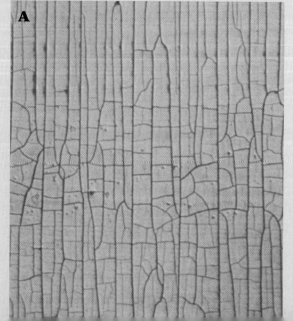
A

B

TIPS

- Repair splits in wood siding with exterior wood filler; press together, and remove excess glue. Reinforce repair with galvanized deck screws.

- Repair small holes and gouges in wood siding with exterior wood filler. Allow to dry, and sand smooth.

- Repair metal and vinyl siding with paintable exterior caulking before painting.

- Repair cracks in stucco, using concrete or stucco patch. Overfill the crack, then feather it out to blend with the area.

- Seal seams, open joints, and gaps around doors and windows, using paintable caulking.

When all repairs, scraping, and sanding are finished, wash down the exterior walls with a TSP solution, using a scrub brush attached to a long handle, or power wash. Rinse thoroughly with a sharp stream from your garden hose. Let the surface dry completely before you begin priming. Apply paint within three days of preparation.

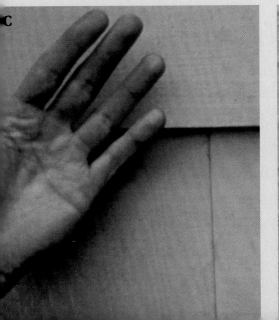
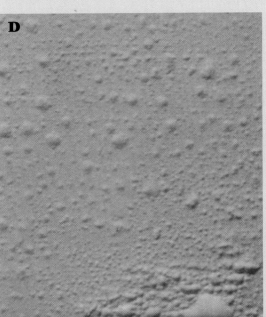

Unless you have a large crew helping you, chances are your exterior paint project will take you several days or weeks to complete. The weather and the number of daylight hours available to you are your main concerns. Perfect conditions for painting are a partly cloudy day with a light breeze, pleasant temperatures, and low humidity.

weather conditions

TIPS

• When time is limited, plan to finish at least one complete wall at a time.

• Plan the day so that you are never painting in direct sunlight. The intense heat may cause the paint to dry too fast, causing blistering and peeling and a paint job that doesn't last.

• Stop painting so that the surface has time to dry before evening dew sets in. Never paint when you are expecting rain or high humidity within 24 hours. The dampness causes premature peeling and may cause latex paint to discolour.

• Never paint when the temperature will fall below 10°C (50°F) within 24 hours, or the paint will not cure properly and may peel and/or discolour.

• Avoid windy conditions, when dirt, bugs, and leaves may be blown into your fresh paint and your paint may dry too quickly.

Heins Creek   Huntsville

Priming over the existing colour on eaves and downspouts makes the transition to a lighter colour much easier. This muted green monochromatic scheme uses the darker value for the trim.

prime time

Priming is a crucial step in your exterior painting project. The right primer does all these things:

- seals the surface, preventing peeling, rusting, and bleed-through

- prevents areas of uneven gloss

- adds years to the life of the paint

- helps the paint adhere better

- can save you from having to apply additional coats of paint

Convinced? Then it's just a matter of selecting the right primers for your project. What's right for your wood siding isn't right for your eaves and downspouts. Since primers are not intended to withstand the elements for long, plan to paint soon after priming.

ON THIS SURFACE	USE THIS PRIMER
old alkyd paint or chalky surface	exterior alkyd primer
old latex paint	exterior acrylic latex or alkyd primer
bare wood	exterior alkyd or latex primer
knots, graffiti, water and smoke stains	stain-barrier primer
vinyl or aluminum siding	exterior acrylic latex primer
galvanized metal	galvanized metal primer or exterior acrylic latex primer

Canso Sky   Dijon

The warm yellow accent colour on the shutters enhances the cool blue colour used for the siding. To complete this triadic scheme, perhaps a muted magenta could be painted on the front door.

75

surfaces &techniques

Whether your home's exterior is wood, vinyl or aluminum lap siding, stucco, or shingles, there are painting tools and techniques designed for you. Some general painting tips apply, no matter which category you fall into:

Exterior paints include acrylic latex in flat, semi-gloss, and gloss finishes, and alkyd paint in gloss finish. Most often exterior walls are painted with flat or semi-gloss paint; soffit, fascia, window and door trim, and exterior doors are usually painted with a semi-gloss or gloss finish.

In this monochromatic scheme, two pale muted green colours are accented by a purer green.

Heins Creek   Fluffy Duvet   Shrub

lap siding

techniques

1. Working on several rows within your reach, paint the narrow bottom edges. Use a wide paintbrush held flat against the siding.

2. Paint the broad faces of those same rows,

painting in long horizontal strokes and working from the top row down.

3. Repeat steps 1 and 2 in each adjacent section until the wall is finished.

board & batten siding

techniques

1. Paint the edges and then the faces of the battens (the narrow boards), using a narrow paintbrush.

2. Paint wide boards using a wide paintbrush, pad, or roller with a deep nap.

techniques

1. For relatively smooth surfaces, paint the narrow bottom edges of the rows within your reach, using a wide brush held flat against the wall.

2. Paint the flat surfaces in vertical strokes, using a large exterior painting pad or a 3" to 4" (7.5 to 10 cm) brush.

3. Repeat steps 1 and 2 in each adjacent section until the wall is finished.

For very rough surfaces, apply the paint with a rough-surface painter, which looks like a scrub brush, or use a paint sprayer.

trim

techniques

Face-off method. Paint the outer edges of the trim when you paint the siding, using the exterior wall paint. When all the walls are finished, apply the trim paint to the face and inner surfaces (next to windows and doors) of all the trim.

Wrap method. Paint all areas of the trim, including the edge next to the siding, with the trim paint.

techniques

1. Paint relatively smooth stucco using a deep-nap roller. Follow the general directions for painting with rollers on page 62.

2. Touch up irregular surface areas with a paintbrush, if necessary.

Apply paint to rough stucco using a paint sprayer.

FOR THIS SURFACE	SELECT THIS PAINT
new wood (primed)	flat latex, semi-gloss latex, gloss latex, or gloss alkyd
painted wood	flat latex, semi-gloss latex, gloss latex, or gloss alkyd
stained wood	gloss latex or gloss alkyd
trim and doors	semi-gloss latex, gloss latex, or gloss alkyd
aluminum siding	flat latex or semi-gloss latex
vinyl siding	flat latex or semi-gloss latex
stucco	flat latex
brick	flat latex
primed metal	semi-gloss latex, gloss latex, or gloss alkyd

INDEX